NEBS
MANAGEMENT
DEVELOPMENT

SUPER **SERIES**

THIRD EDITION
Managing Resources

Working with Budgets

Published for

&**NEBS** Management *by*

**Pergamon
Open
Learning**

Pergamon Open Learning
An imprint of Butterworth-Heinemann
Linacre House, Jordan Hill, Oxford OX2 8DP
A division of Reed Educational and Professional Publishing Ltd

℞ A member of the Reed Elsevier plc group

OXFORD BOSTON JOHANNESBURG
MELBOURNE NEW DELHI SINGAPORE

First published 1986
Second edition 1991
Third edition 1997

British Library Cataloguing in Publication Data
A catalogue record for this book is available from the British Library

ISBN 0 7506 3306 9

NEBS Management Project Manager: Diana Thomas
Author: Raymond Taylor
Editor: Ian Bloor
Series Editor: Diana Thomas
Based on previous material by: Joe Johnson and Alastair Clelland
Composition by Genesis Typesetting, Rochester, Kent
Printed and bound in Great Britain

Contents

Workbook introduction

Here are the workbook titles in each module which link with *Working with Budgets*, should you wish to extend your study to other Super Series workbooks. There is a brief description of each workbook in the User Guide.

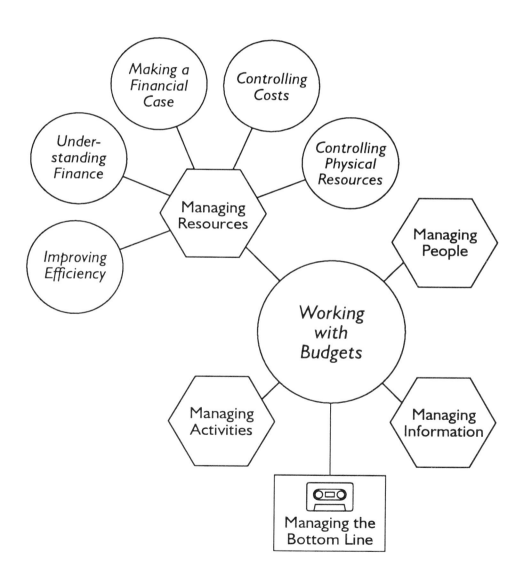

2 S/NVQ links

This workbook relates to the following elements:

B1.1 Make recommendations for the use of resources
B1.2 Contribute to the control of resources
D1.1 Gather required information
D1.2 Inform and advise others

It will also help you to develop the following Personal Competences:

- searching for information;
- thinking and taking decisions.

3 Workbook objectives

You will have plans for your career and your private life. There are things you will want to do today, tomorrow, next week, next year. And because most events and activities cost money, you will know that it's usually necessary to make financial plans to achieve your aims.

The same principles are relevant at work. Your organization has aims and objectives with financial implications and these are identified by using budgets.

By preparing budgets which allocate money to specific purposes, an organization seeks to gain more control over its activities. Careful monitoring then helps to ensure that spending is kept within bounds. Budgets are considered an essential tool by organizations in the management of their affairs.

As a line manager at work, you will probably have a responsibility to meet budgetary targets, and to provide information for budget preparation. This workbook is intended to guide you in those tasks, and to increase your understanding of budgets.

3.1 Objectives

When you have completed this workbook you will be better able to:

- describe what a budget is;
- provide the information required to prepare budgets;
- understand how budgets are used;
- use some budgetary control techniques.

4 Activity planner

The following Activities require some planning so you may want to look at these now.

- Activity 7   In which you look at budget deviations
- Activity 25   Which covers budget variances
- Activity 38   Which covers control of resources

Some or all of these Activities may provide the basis of evidence for your S/NVQ portfolio. All portfolio activities and the Work-based assignment are sign posted with this icon.

Portfolio of evidence

The icon states the elements to which the portfolio activities and Work-based assignment relate.

The Work-based assignment (on page 64) suggests that you speak to your manager, finance director or to your colleagues in the accounts office about the way in which budgets are used in your organization. You might like to start thinking now about who to approach and arrange to speak with them.

Session A What is a budget?

1 Introduction

How would you feel if you were never sure if you would be paid on pay-day or not?

To ensure that you do get paid on the right day, your organization needs to plan and to control the ways in which it spends and receives money so that enough cash is available to pay wages and salaries when due. The organization draws up a plan indicating how it expects money to flow in and out. This plan is better known as a budget.

You probably do the same at home, planning how to use your income. You budget, your employer prepares a budget and, of course, the country as a whole budgets.

Each year, the Chancellor of the Exchequer presents a Budget to Parliament. Its aim is to achieve things which are part of the government's policy on how best to run the country.

Activity 1

3 mins

Write down three things the Chancellor might try to achieve through the annual Budget.

_____

_____

_____

Typical examples might be to:

- reduce inflation;
- combat unemployment;
- help small businesses;
- put defence or social services policies into action;
- win the next election!

Whatever plans and policies the government has, they all have to be financed. The Budget is all about getting hold of and using money.

I

To achieve this, the Chancellor might introduce policies to:

■ cut or tighten control over major items of expenditure;
■ switch expenditure and resources from one item to another;
■ use a variety of financial incentives and penalties.

The national Budget requires a lot of analysis, planning negotiations and juggling with resources. It covers both national income and national expenditure. All budgets work in similar ways; just the amounts involved differ.

2 The purpose of budgets

Think about your own workplace for a moment. Your workteam may be earning income through the sales it achieves or the services it supplies.

Or it might be contributing in one or two other ways:

directly, by purchasing, manufacturing or processing materials, to produce goods that are sold	**indirectly**, by such things as designing, controlling, maintaining equipment, or providing services to customers or other workteams

Whatever it does, your workteam is certain to incur expenditure (costs), in doing its job, and to receive income. Almost certainly, the organization you belong to will have prepared a budget for its expenditure, which of course must be related to its expected income.

A budget can be described as:

'a quantitative plan of action prepared in advance of a defined period of time'.

Let's look at this definition more closely.

■ A budget is quantitative.

That means it must be stated in figures; in practice this usually means in sums of money. A general statement of what you intend to do may be useful, but it's not a budget.

■ A budget is prepared in advance.

A budget must be drawn up *before* the period to which it refers. Figures produced during or after the period may be important, but they are not part of a budget.

- A budget relates to a particular period.

  Budgets are drawn up for a certain specific period (often, though not always, one year). An open-ended financial plan for the future isn't a budget.

- A budget is a plan of action.

  This is perhaps the most important point of all. A budget can't be a definite statement of fact, because it relates to something which hasn't happened yet.

Conditions may change during the budget period, which means the budget will be inaccurate. Like all plans, budgets seldom turn out to be totally correct predictions of the future. Even so, they can still be useful in guiding the actions of those using them. This guidance role is very important.

Of course, you must know what you are trying to achieve before planning. Everything else depends on that.

'Knowing what to achieve' is referred to in business as an **objective**.

The objectives of your workplace will depend to some extent on what kind of organization it is and may be short, medium or long term. Manufacturing industries, for example, have to make a profit. Local government services have to provide a certain level of service. A nationalized industry may be required to achieve a planned return on capital invested.

Some other examples of objectives are:

- to make a profit of 30 per cent on a certain product;
- to increase the share of the market by 5 per cent for a certain product;
- to improve service to the public in certain areas.
- to survive commercially for a financial year. (this one is particularly relevant to new, small businesses.)

To achieve any of these needs planning and will probably involve the production of budgets.

Activity 2

3 mins

Write down **two** different kinds of budget that are used in your organization to meet its objectives. One example would be a sales budget.

_____

_____

The budgets listed below are all common types. Perhaps your suggestions are among them, though you could well have thought of others too.

- sales budget
- production budget
- research and development budget
- training budget
- departmental costs budget
- cash budget.

All budgets are important although it is arguable that the cash budget is most important because without cash a business is in trouble.

Let's look briefly at sales budgets and cash budgets, to make sure we understand what they mean.

In a **sales budget**, a forecast is made of the sales the company will make during the relevant period. This may be broken down by section or department. Knowing how much you will sell is essential, in order to decide how much raw materials you will buy, how many employees you will need, and so on.

In a **cash budget** the accountant will forecast:

- what cash will be received and paid out during the budget period;
- the timing of receipts and payments;
- the bank balance or overdraft for each month.

The cash budget is especially important for small, newly established businesses.

Activity 3

2 mins

Who do you think would expect to see the cash budget of a newly established business? Write down **one** suggestion.

_____

_____

EXTENSION I
Assignment 14 in this book gives illustrations of the situations faced by businesses that have and have not prepared a cash budget.

You may have thought of a number of possibilities. The one I had in mind was the bank manager who will want to examine the cash forecasts of a new business, and will almost certainly insist on a cash budget before authorizing a loan for a new business.

However, I don't want to give the impression that it is only new, small businesses which find cash budgets important. Organizations, large and small, use them, and so do charities and social clubs.

4

3 Beginning a budget

How a budget is actually produced and the role that you, as a line manager, have in producing it, is something we'll explore in Session B. For the moment, let's just think about the beginning of the budget process.

Let's begin with manufacturing industry – in a business which makes and sells something.

We need first to identify the critical factor which influences all the budgets in a certain workplace. The factor influences all other budgets, and is called the **key** or **limiting budget factor**.

In practice:

■ the **sales budget** is the commonest limiting budget factor in established commercial businesses;
■ the **cash budget** is the commonest limiting budget factor in newly established small businesses.

Sometimes the **production budget** is the limiting budget factor, although this is less common.

Activity 4

In each of the following situations, the key budget – the one on which other budgets will depend – will have to be produced first. To remind you, in a manufacturing company, this may be a **cash**, **sales** or **production** budget. Look at each situation and decide which is the key budget for each.

Firm A exists in a highly competitive market and currently sells 500 units per month. It plans to increase this to 600 units per month in the coming year and, in fact, has the capacity to produce 750 units per month.	Cash ☐ Sales ☐ Production ☐
Firm B is the sole supplier of a specialist component. It can sell all it produces and more.	Cash ☐ Sales ☐ Production ☐
Firm C is a small business with a large overdraft. It is currently owed a great deal of money, and its bank insists that the overdraft cannot be extended.	Cash ☐ Sales ☐ Production ☐
Firm D is a haulage contractor with a fleet of ten lorries on the road that has been offered a contract to transport twelve lorry-loads of goods to Southern Europe on a weekly basis. The firm cannot afford to purchase additional lorries.	Cash ☐ Sales ☐ Production ☐

EXTENSION 2
Pages 135–8
provide useful
advice on
identifying the key
or limiting factor.

Here is what I would say is the key budget, on which all other budgets would depend, for each of these firms:

- For Firm A, it's a sales budget. The firm must sell more. Everything else, including production, will follow from that.

- For Firm B, it's a production budget. The firm has to produce more. If it achieves this then extra sales will follow.

- For Firm C, it's a cash budget. The most important thing is for the firm to earn cash at the moment. This might even mean that the firm would have to refuse a potentially profitable contract if it didn't bring in cash quickly enough.

- For Firm D, the key is the cash budget because the firm does not have enough cash to buy more lorries to provide the transport service offered.

4 The advantages of budgets

Some people think of a budget as something that restricts what we want or need to do. It certainly can be very frustrating when the constraints of a budget, drawn up by accountants who (you may feel) have no understanding of your problems, prevents you from taking certain actions in your job.

See if you recognize any of the following situations or something similar.

- The training budget of a hospital has been spent. A nursing sister is refused permission to go on a course to learn how to use a new piece of equipment for monitoring heart disease. She is concerned because she feels that patient care may suffer.

- The entertainments budget of a growing electronics firm is exhausted. The sales manager is unable to offer the kind of hospitality he would like to a visiting trade delegation from Saudi Arabia. No orders are won.

- The overtime budget of a shipbuilding company is already overspent. No new overtime is authorized and the ship ends up three months late to the customer. Massive penalties result.

- The departmental budget in the chemistry department of a university is underspent with one month of the financial year to go. The professor authorizes a spending spree to ensure his budget is not cut next year. Unneeded equipment which is rarely if ever used is purchased.

Having a plan, which is all the budget is, can only be a good thing. In these examples, the budgets themselves were not to blame for the unfortunate results. So what went wrong?

Activity 5

6 mins

Write down any ideas you have about who or what was responsible for the problems arising in any of the situations described above.

_____

_____

_____

_____

> A budget is only a plan and provides guidance. Budgets should not be rigidly kept to as an excuse for not managing. Sometimes an adaptation of a plan is more sensible.

You may have noted a number of possibilities but perhaps we can narrow them down to:

- an over-rigid view of how the budgets should be enforced has been taken – this seems likely to be the case in the first and second examples;
- the budgets have been badly produced and managed, particularly the third and fourth examples.

If necessary, senior management usually have authority to over-ride a budget if they consider it would be economically worthwhile to do so. For example, it might be appropriate to intervene to prevent the company having to pay contract penalties for late delivery, because its overtime budget is overspent. They might achieve this by transferring savings made in one budget to another, a process known as **virement**.

Budgets are intended to be beneficial.

It is when they are badly produced or managed, that they can have undesirable consequences.

Having seen the downside of poor budgeting practice, let us look at the benefits of good budget practice.

Organizations benefit in a number of areas through budgeting.

- Co-ordination and teamwork

The process of budgeting means that management at all levels and in different departments are given the opportunity to meet, discuss and relate their targets to each other. Organizations are most successful if everyone works together to meet common goals rather than each manager acting selfishly to build their own empires.

The co-ordination process helps managers get an understanding of how each activity relates to the whole, which is very important for them and for the business. It would be pointless, for example, for the sales manager to plan a 10 per cent increase if the production manager is aiming for a 5 per cent cutback.

7

■ Communication

In order to work to a budget, people have to **know** what is possible or impossible in their own workplace.

Budgeting encourages management at all levels to talk to one another about the company's policies and the target they are aiming for. Again this builds teamwork; people working for each other and for their organizations.

■ Planning

As we've seen, planning is at the heart of a budgeting system. Using a budgeting system means that managers and supervisors have to use formal procedures to think about the future, instead of muddling along from one day to the next. It also means that thought is given to the level of performance expected in every part of the organization.

> Budgetary control is a formal way of delegating responsibility.

■ Control

The whole point of a budget is to influence the direction the organization is taking. For a budget to be of value,

the actual outcome must be regularly compared with the planned outcome.

If the two don't match up, then controls can be used to take appropriate action. Without a plan there is no yardstick to measure what's happening; any controls, therefore, are fairly random.

The idea of a system of budgets is to get a clearer picture of planned activities and to make departments and individuals responsible for spending and cost control in their own areas. In this way, the strengths of sections and departments can be capitalized on, and ways found to overcome any weaknesses.

■ Motivation

The more people are involved at every level in setting up a budget, and in the planning and control that goes with it, the more they understand and support what the organization is trying to achieve. Involvement is an important motivating factor at any level.

All these points are valid, but the two most important purposes of budgets are **planning** and **control**. The planning process enables controls to be set into place.

Let's explore the idea of budgetary controls a little further.

5 Using budgetary control

Budgetary control is a very useful management tool. It should enable a manager or supervisor to do his or her job more effectively, without detracting from individual skill or flexibility.

Control must be an active process.

Activity 6

4 mins

One important question for a manager, which budgets should help to provide the answer to, is: 'Is my workteam (or section, or department) keeping its spending within agreed limits?'

Can you think of at least **one** other question to which a manager or supervisor might want to know the answer, and which budgets should help provide?

_____

_____

_____

You may have thought of several possible questions. Perhaps you included the following.

■ 'Are we reaching agreed targets?'
■ 'If we are not reaching agreed spending limits or agreed targets, where are we falling down, and for what reasons?'
■ 'What can I do to try to improve the performance of my team?'
■ 'Do events suggest that the budget needs to be modified?'

By monitoring actual results against budgets, control is improved. You should be able to identify problems and take action quickly and there is less incentive just to let matters slide.

No budget is perfect. Unforeseen circumstances do arise. For example, a competitor may suddenly bring out a new product, the bottom may drop out of a market or we may have a strike on our hands. Any number of events can make budgeted figures less accurate, some within the control of managers, some not.

Activity 7

5
mins

This Activity may provide the basis of appropriate evidence for your S/NVQ portfolio. If you are intending to take this course of action, it might be better to write your answers on separate sheets of paper.

Think about your own job.

Write down **two** factors why your workteam might deviate from its budget, which are largely **within** your control.

_____

_____

_____

_____

Now write down **two** factors that might make your workteam deviate from its budget, which are largely **outside** your control.

_____

_____

_____

_____

Your response will be related to your own job.

■ As factors within your control you might have put down answers such as faulty work, bad timekeeping by employees, inefficient organization of the department, new staff not inducted properly and so on.

■ Factors likely to be outside a line manager's control are the hold-up of supplies, teething problems with new products or systems, shortages of staff and so forth.

Because there are many ways in which a budget can become inaccurate, an organization must try to obtain the best possible information at the time of budgeting. It should look to see, for instance, what it has achieved in the past, and what its costs actually are.

Self-assessment 1

1 A properly drawn-up budget can be described as having **four** important features. Identify all four features.

_____

_____

_____

_____

_____

_____

_____

_____

2 Write down **two** initial uses for budgets at the time when they are drawn up.

_____

_____

_____

_____

3 Fill in the missing words in the following sentences.

a Budgets are largely a waste of time unless they are actively _____ in order to see whether the organization is_____ its targets and keeping within its limits.

b We use the term _____ _____ to cover the use of budgets to help an organization control its progress towards what it has set out to achieve.

c A budget will not be useful to an organization if it is managed so _____ that it does not permit some degree of flexibility.

Answers to these questions can be found on pages 71–2.

6 Summary

■ A budget is a **plan** usually described in financial terms, drawn up to meet certain objectives in the workplace.

■ The starting point in producing a budget is to determine the **key** or **limiting factor** which influences all other budgets. This will often be the sales budget.

■ **Control** is central to the budgeting process. The system of using budgets and comparing actual and budgeted results to control progress towards objectives is **budgetary control**.

■ Budgeting should never be so inflexible as to prevent sensible decisions being taken.

■ Budgets can also help to improve:

  ■ co-ordination;
  ■ communication;
  ■ motivation.

■ Good budgeting should help an organization meet its goals and ensure that everyone works together towards those goals.

Session B Preparing budgets

1 Introduction

In Session A, we saw that the budget is a financial plan, crucial to the successful management of any organization in a given period. Clearly, preparing the budget needs a great deal of carefully co-ordinated information from different people.

You looked at some poor budgeting techniques earlier and this flows through to provision of information too. You can see examples of bad budgeting every year as government ministers try to get a larger share of tax revenues:

- there will be scare tactics about people dying if health budgets are cut;
- you will hear that jobs will be lost if local authorities and schools do not get more money;
- reports will say that crime will be rife if the police do not receive a few more million pounds.

Every minister fights for their own share of the national cake without necessarily ensuring the good of the nation as a whole. However, as different departments appear to have limitless demands and the government has scarce resources, it is perhaps not surprizing that extreme tactics are used.

In this session you will see how budgets are put together and look at the roles of different people in the process. You will also study useful techniques to follow in drawing up budgets.

2 The budget committee

The preparation of the budget is often the responsibility of a **budget committee**, whose chairperson is usually a senior manager. Sometimes the chairperson may even be the top person in the organization – the managing director, chief executive, Chancellor of the Exchequer, or whatever his or her particular title happens to be.

All the main functions or areas of responsibility in the workplace should be represented on a budget committee.

13

Activity 8

Think about your own workplace.

Jot down the job titles of **three** of the people whom you would expect to represent major areas of responsibility on your budget committee.

_____

_____

_____

EXTENSION 3
Chapter 6 looks at the role of management in budget setting.

Different organizations work in different ways so your answers to this Activity are likely to vary from those of others studying this workbook. However, here is my list of some of the people I would expect to find on a budget committee in a manufacturing company.

- general manager (chairman)
- company secretary
- sales manager
- production manager
- administration manager
- purchasing manager
- personnel manager
- chief accountant.

Each member of the committee will have the task of producing forecasts for his or her own area of responsibility. So:

- the sales manager will forecast how much he or she expects to be able to sell, and what the selling price should be for each product item;
- the production manager will forecast what production levels are possible.

In a small company, the budget forecast may be made by only two or three managers – or even, perhaps, one person working alone, burning the midnight oil!

The people involved would have different titles in other industries. For instance, if we take the example of a design consultancy, the budget committee might comprise:

- partner-proprietors
- head of design
- head of marketing and sales
- human resources manager
- finance manager.

People on a budget committee provide forecasts in their own areas of responsibility.

- The administration manager will need to forecast the costs of administration and changes in the cost of items such as rent and rates.
- The purchasing manager will forecast the costs of materials in the coming period, including raw materials and all the equipment and supplies the business needs to function.
- The personnel or human resources manager will forecast the staffing needed to operate the coming period and the costs of keeping, taking on or shedding staff. The cost of staff will be affected by current pay negotiations in the company's particular industry and in the country as a whole.
- The head of design will forecast the resources needed to provide work of appropriate quality to meet the goals set by the business owners in the forthcoming period.
- The chief accountant or finance manager will advise on the implications of whatever is planned on the company's cash position and provide other departments with information about past costs and levels of performance. The cost of borrowing varies widely, sometimes from month to month, and there are all sorts of other financial constraints or incentives (such as government grants) which may affect the company's plans.

The chief accountant will also have the job of producing the **master budget**, which brings together all the other budgets, and which in a business organization provides a forecast of the profit which the company can expect to make.

A non-profit-making organization such as a hospital will show in its master budget how it plans to operate within the limits of its grant or other income it has received.

Most large organizations produce a budget manual which tells everybody involved in the budget what is required and how to collect and present the information.

The budget committee start by forecasting the critical elements of the budget, in terms of money or other quantities, as far as they are able. These will include such things as:

- levels of sales;
- planned increase or decrease of stock;
- levels of production needed to meet any changes planned in sales and stocks.

Sometimes these critical elements will fit together well. At other times, departments may need to revise their plans so that, say, sales levels are reduced to allow for lower production or insufficient cash to pay for stock.

Try this example of the sort for forecasting which has to take place.

Activity 9

Sahid Enterprises Ltd currently produce 10,000 lighting components in a year. At a meeting in December the budget committee agree that sales in the coming year should be 14,000 components, and the stock levels should be reduced from 3000 to 2000 components by the end of the year.

Calculate the planned production level for the coming year.

_____

_____

You should have calculated the planned production level at 13,000 units:

sales (14,000) – planned decrease in stock levels (1000)

= production level needed (13,000)

In practice, the various factors which have to be pulled together and the number and complexity of the calculations is much greater than this. However, the general idea is the same.

If you work in an organization whose main purpose is to provide a service (a hospital or a library for instance), you are likely to look at things differently.

Budgets are prepared in a slightly different way in organizations which set out to make a profit, compared with those which don't. We'll look at way different organizations go about obtaining information for budgets and putting them together.

3 Gathering and co-ordinating information

3.1 Preparation of sales estimates

You have seen that the **key** or **limiting** factor has to be worked out first, as it is the factor on which all other budgets depend. In profit-seeking businesses the limiting factor is usually sales.

Thus the sales department forecast has to be made before colleagues in purchasing or production can make theirs. Having said that, though, we've seen that different functions of the company have to work closely to prepare budgets. It's no use sales planning to sell far more than production can produce, or production planning to make more than sales can sell.

The sales manager (or whoever prepares the sales budget) has a special responsibility: to determine the sales forecast for the coming year as accurately as possible. If the sales manager is wrong, everybody else's budget will be wrong too.

Information can be gathered by internal and external methods:

- **Internal methods**

  - Reports from your area sales managers and sales representatives.
  - Statistical analysis of past sales records to identify trends which seem likely to continue.

- **External methods**

  - Market research information about customer's likes and dislikes and about what competitors are doing.
  - Information about the general economic climate, which may tell you whether people are likely to be spending more or less money on, say, sweets and chocolates.

Using **internal methods** entails finding out information from within the company's own records. You may even be able to arrive at your forecast simply by summing up individual sales representatives' forecasts.

Using **external methods** involves going outside the company. You may use your own staff to research some of this information, and you may glean some from official publications.

Activity 10

5 mins

EXTENSION 3
Chapter 4 expands on the idea of who provides the figures for budgets.

Suggest **one** possible benefit of internal methods and **one** possible disadvantage.

_____

_____

_____

_____

There is not necessarily one right answer to this Activity but this is what springs to mind.

- One major benefit of internal methods is that they involve a lot of people at all levels in the budget process. Provided they understand what they're doing and why, and realize how important it is, they can make people feel more interested in and committed to the company and the job.

■ The major disadvantage of internal methods is that they only reflect what is happening inside the company. They don't take into account changes in economic conditions, or what the competition is doing. Estimates produced by internal methods only may tend to be over-optimistic.

A good sales forecast may be based on an **internal** forecast which is adjusted at a senior level to take account of available **external** data.

3.2 The budget

Once the important estimates, particularly sales, have been made, other things start to fall into place. The budget committee can go on to produce the rest of the budget, described in money terms.

We've already worked out that, once the sales estimate is known and any increases or decreases in stock have been planned, it's possible to produce the production budget. What comes next?

Activity 11

Here is a diagram of the budgets prepared so far and a list of some of the remaining budgets which still have to be prepared. Fill in the budget you think should follow next in the preparation sequence from the list of budgets still to be prepared:

■ departmental expense budget
■ cash budget
■ budgeted profit and loss account
■ resources budget.

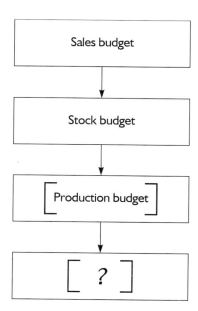

Once you've prepared the production budget and decided what production levels are planned in the coming year, you will have to plan the resources you need to meet these levels. Thus, the resources budget comes next in the sequence. In practice, this involves preparing three separate budgets for the following production costs.

- **Machine use:** the operating hours required on each machine or group of machines and the cost of those hours.
- **Material usage:** required quantities and costs of all materials needed to meet planned production levels.
- **Labour:** the number of person hours needed on production to meet production targets and the cost of those hours.

If you work in a manufacturing industry, this may well be very much on your territory. As a line manager, you probably have a key role in this area of resource planning and control.

Activity 12

6 mins

Identify **two** consequences of poor supervision in each of the three main resource budget areas.

Machine use

_____

_____

Material usage

_____

_____

Labour

_____

_____

There may be a wide range of consequences. Certainly poor supervision may lead to overspending. Here are just some of the consequences you may have noted.

- Poor supervision of **machine use** could lead to:

  - more breakdowns
  - more idle time
  - higher maintenance costs
  - more scrap.

19

- Poor supervision of **material usage** could lead to:

  - more scrap
  - pilferage
  - bottle-necks in production or idle time.

- Poor supervision of **labour** could lead to:

  - low quality work or more scrap
  - poor timekeeping
  - increased overtime budget.

Now let's see how preparing the resources budget leads to the next budget in the sequence by working through an example.

Activity 13

4 mins

- Unique Windows Ltd manufacture double-glazed windows for which the basic materials are timber and glass.

  Budget sales for the coming year are 8000 units.

  Stock at the beginning of the year is 1500 complete units, but the production controller believes this level of stock is too high and plans to reduce stocks to 600 complete units by the end of the year.

Complete the calculation for the production needed in the coming year.

Budget sales

Less stock adjustment

Required production

Here's the completed calculation.

Budget sales   8000

Less stock adjustment   900 (1500 − 600)

Required production   7100

Now let's add to that information.

- A standard window uses:

- 5 m² glass, which costs £18 per square metre;
- 10 m timber, which costs £12 per metre.

Activity 14

4 mins

Work out what will be the total materials usage, and the cost for timber and glass to meet the required production of 7,100 standard windows.

Glass usage = 7100 × 5 m², which costs _____ × £18

= £ _____

Timber usage = 7100 × 10 m, which costs _____ × £12

= £ _____

In order to produce 7100 units the materials usage would be:

Glass usage = 7100 × 5 m², which costs 35,500 × £18 = £639,000;

Timber usage = 7100 × 10 m, which costs 71,000 × £12 = £852,000.

Now we know how much material usage is planned we can decide how much will have to be bought in. So the next budget to be prepared is the **raw material stock budget**, which will plan for the actual materials to be purchased.

- Unique Windows Ltd has these opening stock levels at the beginning of the year:

- 5000 m² of glass;
- 6800 m of timber.

They plan to reduce stock levels held and the planned closing stock levels are:

- 3000 m² of glass;
- 6000 m of timber.

To calculate the quantity and cost of the glass it needs to purchase we do the following calculation.

Usage	35,500 m²
Add stock required at close	3,000 m²
Deduct stock at beginning	(5,000) m²
Budgeted purchase	33,500 × £18 = £603,000

You see that we've used the same principles as when we calculated the production level required, by taking the sales figure and adjusting it by the difference between the opening and closing stock figure.

Activity 15

4 mins

Work out in the same way the quantity and cost of the timber which will have to be purchased.

Usage = _____ m

Add stock required at close = _____ m

Deduct stock at beginning = _____ m

Budgeted purchase = _____ × £ _____

= £ _____

Here is the completed calculation to compare with yours.

Usage	= 71,000 m
Add stock required at close	= 6,000 m
Deduct stock at beginning	= (6,800) m
Budgeted purchase	= 70,200 m × £12 = £842,400

We've just followed through one part of the resources budget, consisting of the **materials usage budget**, **raw material stock budget** and **materials purchase budget**.

But don't forget that the resources budget must also contain the plan for the use of machines and labour, as well as the materials needed, to meet planned production levels. So calculations like the one we have just been looking at will also have to be carried out for machine use and labour. These will, in turn, lead on to other related budgets.

Try the next Activity to ensure that you have grasped the order of budgets so far.

Activity 16

Fill in the blanks below to show the order in which budgets for Unique Windows Ltd are prepared

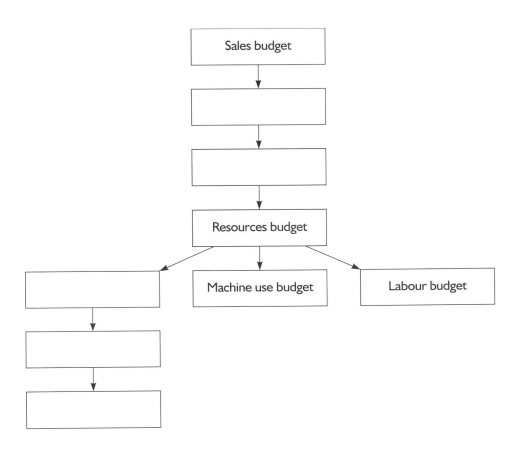

The answer to this Activity can be found on page 74.

We said earlier that budget preparation is different in some respects if you are not in the business of manufacturing something. So let's now have a look at the parallel stages of budget preparation in organizations that offer some kind of service.

4 Service industries

A service industry may provide transport, for instance, or supply gas or electricity, or it may offer medical services. There are many thousands of service organizations which we all depend on.

Private service industries have to make a profit in order to stay in business, an example is a haulage contractor who transports goods manufactured by other businesses. Some public organizations (NHS hospitals, for instance) do not expect to make a profit, but have to plan to provide the best service they can within the money they are allocated. In the new public sector, internal and other markets have been given more significance. This means that the budgeting process in the public sector is more or less identical to the approach in the private sector.

Most service organizations do not need a finished stock budget or a production budget. However, their budgeting process is equally important to them.

Let's look first at the budget development for Tim Hawkins, haulage contractor.

■ Tim starts at the same point as a manufacturer – estimating sales in the coming period. In his case, the sales will be the number of contracts to carry goods that Tim thinks he can win.

Activity 17

2 mins

Having determined the sales budget, what do you think will be the next stage in budget preparation for Tim Hawkins' business?

_____

_____

I hope you decided that the next stage was to plan the resources required to meet planned sales: how many lorries, how many drivers etc.

So Tim's budget sequence might look something like this.

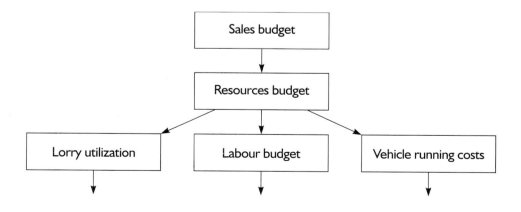

Activity 18

2 mins

What might Tim Hawkins, the haulage contractor, do if his present resources were insufficient to meet budgeted sales? Write down **two** suggestions.

_____

_____

He could do a number of things including:

- purchasing or hiring more lorries;
- using his existing fleet of lorries and drivers more efficiently;
- refusing the contracts that he couldn't meet with his present resources.

If he had more resources than he needed to meet budgeted sales, on the other hand, he might decide to:

- lay off staff;
- dispose of surplus lorries;
- reduce his prices to attract business.

Any or all of these decisions would have to be tackled at his next stage of budget preparation.

National Health Service trusts and hospitals, too, are clearly concerned with making the best use of available resources, but in their case the limiting factor is not usually their equivalent of 'sales', the demand for beds from sick patients. It is instead the allocation of resources, much of which the hospitals receive from central government, even if that is through the internal market for health through General Practitioners.

Hospitals rarely find they have too many resources available, as the demand for health care appears to grow continually. Hospitals do make cuts in their budgets, but this is usually due to a cut in the reduced basic availability of resources and funds, rather than because demand is reduced.

In a hospital, the number of beds can be used as a limiting factor. An estimate can be made as to the occupancy or utilization of each bed through the year. This is similar to the way in which hotels budget, although basic cost information about the length of stay of a variety of patients is more complex than business or holiday visitors to a hotel. A private hospital will budget on bed occupancy and the price paid for bed use against the costs of providing care.

5 Departmental budgets

Having looked at what happens in manufacturing and service industries separately, we can now look at what happens inside organizations, so far as budgeting is concerned. Although there will be some variation in details, departmental budget preparation is similar in most types of organization.

At the same time as the major budgets are being produced, managers and supervisors in every department are having to estimate how much it will cost them to carry out their responsibilities in the coming period.

Many of us provide a sort of back-up service to the main function of the business we're in. Thus, if a firm makes furniture, the job of departments such as sales, finance, the administration office, the computer section, design, materials testing and so on, can all be regarded as providing back-up services to the manufacturing process. We can even argue that the factory itself provides a back-up service, since it is not directly part of the manufacturing process.

Back-up costs are known as **overheads**.
Sometimes deciding what is, and what is not an overhead, can be quite difficult. Nevertheless, it is very important for any organization to identify overheads and to keep them under control.

To give you an idea of what's involved in preparing departmental budgets in order that a full picture of overheads can be built up, let's look at some examples.

Activity 19

5 mins

- In the Nottinghamshire factory, all lorries delivering materials or taking away finished goods have to get security clearance before coming up to the loading bay of the stores. The factory runs a continuous process, so routine maintenance and factory cleaning has to take place while production is running. This results in as little disruption to the schedule as possible.

This description of activities in a factory contains clues to some of the departmental budgets which will have to be prepared. Suggest **three** of them, and say who you think might be responsible for preparing them.

The information should have made it possible for you to pick out the likely budgets. The titles of the people responsible for preparing different budgets may vary. The overall responsibility would lie with the factory manager.

- Maintenance budget: responsibility of the maintenance engineer.
- Stores budget: responsibility of the stores controller.
- Cleaning budget: responsibility of the domestic services manager.
- Security budget: responsibility of the chief security officer.

Each of these areas will make an important contribution to production, even though it isn't directly part of the production process.

We could repeat this exercise for other functions in any organization. In sales, for example, there may well be:

- an advertising and sales promotion budget;
- a sales staff budget;
- a van fleet maintenance budget; and so on.

In the preparation of an administration budget, there would be budgets for the accounts section, the computer section, secretarial services and personnel services.

You can probably break down any major function in your own workplace in the same way. You can therefore see that the preparation of a departmental budget needs an enormous amount of information and planning from a large number of people.

Although the most senior person in any one function will have overall responsibility for the departmental budget, you or your manager may well have a large degree of responsibility for the budget in your particular area.

Once you started to examine costs in your area, you would find that, as in every other area in your workplace, the nature of your costs varied.

Activity 20

3 mins

■ June Hamilton manages one of a chain of small shops. Some of the costs incurred by her shop are listed below. Some of these costs vary, depending on the amount of business June's shop does, and some stay the same, regardless of how well the business is doing.

Tick the appropriate boxes to identify costs which vary and which remain the same.

	Varies	Stays the same
Rent	☐	☐
Rates	☐	☐
Wages of sales staff	☐	☐
Wages of part-time bookkeeper	☐	☐
Commission on sales	☐	☐
Packaging material	☐	☐
Electricity for lighting and heating	☐	☐
Insurance of the property and the stock	☐	☐

EXTENSION 4
Further advice on determining cost categories is detailed on pages 48–61.

I would say that rent, rates, wages, electricity and insurance would stay the same, regardless of the amount of business June's shop does. Commission on sales and packaging materials vary depending on how much is sold.

Costs which remain the same whether the level of business activity rises or falls are called **fixed costs**.

Costs which vary with changes in the amount of business being done are called **variable costs**.

Distinguishing between fixed and variable costs can sometimes be quite a complex issue.

Clearly if costs vary with business activity, this has implications for budgeting.

Here's an example of the sort of forecast a sales manager might produce to deal with variable costs.

	Pessimistic sales forecast	Expected sales	Optimistic sales forecast
	£3,000,000	£4,000,000	£5,000,000
Overheads	£	£	£
Commission (2%)	60,000	80,000	100,000
Distribution costs (5%)	150,000	200,000	250,000
	210,000	280,000	350,000
Basic salaries (sales staff)	90,000	90,000	90,000
Manager's salary	20,000	20,000	20,000
Sales office costs	30,000	30,000	30,000
	140,000	140,000	140,000
Total overheads	350,000	420,000	490,000
% of sales	11.67%	10.5%	9.8%

Variable costs rise or fall as sales rise. We can see from the forecast above that all distribution costs and all commissions rise as sales rise. These are variable costs; the other costs remain fixed.

Activity 21

4 mins

Look at the sales manager's forecast. Make a note of what happens to overheads as a percentage of sales if the expected level of sales rises.

_____

_____

_____

_____

Because some of the costs are fixed, the overheads as a percentage of sales decline as anticipated sales increase.

It's easy to regard fixed costs as something of a millstone round your neck, particularly if it is difficult to make sales. But, as we see from this example, if business is booming they decrease as a percentage of the total business activity and become less of a worry.

Once all the departmental budgets are prepared, so giving a picture of the overheads requirements for the coming period, they are passed to the finance department for use in the cash budget and the **master budget**.

6 The master budget

As its name suggests, the **master budget** pulls together all the information produced in every department, and becomes the master plan for the coming period against which other departmental budgets have to be adjusted. The master budget comprises the **budgeted profit and loss account** and **budgeted balance sheet**.

Here's an example of the kind of information a budgeted profit and loss account might contain.

■

	Budget	
	£	£
Sales		3,000,000
Less costs of production:		
Factory labour	500,000	
Factory material	500,000	
Factory overheads	250,000	
	1,250,000	
Less cost of stock:		
Opening stock	500,000	
Closing stock	(250,000)	
	250,000	
Less cost of goods sold:		1,500,000
Gross profit		1,500,000
Less non-production expenses:		
Selling and distribution	350,000	
General administration	400,000	
Less overheads:		750,000
Net profit		750,000

You see that in this example, the starting point is the amount of money which the company expects to gain in sales. From this is taken the costs it expects to incur. The resulting figure is the forecast profit of £750,000.

Activity 22

4 mins

Take a look at the budgeted profit and loss account above. List **four** budgets from which the information used in this statement would have been obtained.

_____

_____

_____

_____

There are a variety of options you may have identified. The costs of production would be obtained from the production budget, which would comprise the labour budget, materials usage budget and machine use budget. The stock budget and materials purchase budget would also be necessary to calculate the cost of goods sold.

All sorts of departmental expenses budgets would need to be included in a budgeted profit and loss account. Above, there are selling, distribution and administration overheads.

When it is complete, the master budget will be reported back to the budget committee. If they are not satisfied, the budget team will have to start work again.

Self-assessment 2

1   Complete the following by filling in the missing words.

   a   The _____ or _____ factor is the factor on which all other budgets depend.

   b   A budget committee is usually made up of people who represent major areas of _____ over expenditure.

2   Armot Ltd produces 12,000 tables each year, but in the next year the budget committee agree that sales should increase by 10 per cent for the next year and that stock levels should reduce from 2000 to 1320 units.

   Calculate the planned production level for the forthcoming year.

   _____

   _____

   _____

3   Identify whether the following represent internal or external sources of information for budgeting for a school.

	Internal	External
a Details of birth rates and local housing starts.	☐	☐
b Advice from teachers about new books and equipment needs.	☐	☐
c National pay awards.	☐	☐

4   Identify the areas of poor supervision which lead to each of the following.

	Machine use	Materials usage	Labour
poor timekeeping	☐	☐	☐
breakdowns	☐	☐	☐
pilferage	☐	☐	☐

5   State briefly why organizations maintain departmental budgets.

   _____

   _____

Answers to these questions can be found on page 72.

7 Summary

- Preparing budgets normally requires co-ordination of senior management in a budget committee.

- Estimating sales based on the reports of sales staff and/or external conditions will usually be the starting point of the budget process in organizations that sell goods or services.

- Knowing the allocation of funds is often the starting point in non-profit-seeking organizations.

- Production levels and costs can be determined once sales are estimated.

- The share of expenses (overheads) allocated to departments will be estimated once sales and production levels have been forecast.

- Some expenses will be fixed and some variable. Higher levels of business activity reduces the impact of fixed costs as they are spread over more units.

- If the final profit estimate which is part of the master budget is unsatisfactory, the process must be reviewed.

- Your main role as a line manager in the budget process will probably be in providing information for the budget forecast and resource planning and control.

Session C Using budgets

1 Introduction

Producing a correct and realistic budget takes time. Putting the information together can take you away from your main job of producing or providing a service and make you ask yourself if budgeting is really worth all the expense and effort.

We have seen the benefits, but unless budgets really work they are not worth preparing.

In this final session we look at several ways in which budgets are used and what makes them important especially in terms of planning and control.

As first line manager you will be involved in implementing the budget allocation of your section in detail. You will monitor operations and ensure that your workteam works within budget as far as is possible and will report on any differences from budget.

In this session you will see what costs you can control and which are uncontrollable. Knowing that will help you understand what actions you can take to make best use of the resources at your disposal and how to monitor those resources.

2 Budgetary control

All budgetary control systems follow basically the same steps:

EXTENSION 3
Further aspects of budgetary control are featured in Chapter 11.

- establish agreed budgets;
- report actual results to departmental managers;
- identify where actual performance differs from planned performance (these differences are called **variances**);
- analyse which department or who is responsible for the variances;
- analyse why the variances have happened.

Activity 23

3 mins

■ Acme Machine Tools Ltd prepared budgets for an income from sales (sales revenue) of £2,000,000 in the coming year. In the event, actual sales revenue turns out to be £1,750,000.

Identify **two** possible reasons why you think the variance might have arisen and who you think will be held accountable for the difference from the plan.

You may have thought of a number of possible reasons why the variance came about, but your suggestions can probably be grouped into three main problem areas:

■ sales price had to be lower than was forecast;
■ the amount of goods sold was less than forecast;
■ credit control was poor and goods sold were not paid for.

Of course, these problems would have to be investigated in more depth to find out what was causing them. It might be something like poor delivery dates, low quality or a competitor putting a better product on the market.

As to who would be held accountable or responsible, it will be whoever was responsible for preparing the sales budget, whether that was the sales director, sales manager or whoever. This person may not be directly to blame for the variance, but he or she carries the responsibility for the problem.

In order to monitor what is happening, managers need budgetary control reports which are sent to them periodically, highlighting variances for which they are responsible. Regular control is more likely to prevent major problems at the end of the budget period.

Here is an extract from a budgetary control report for a manufacturing company.

■

	Budget	Actual	Variance	
Sales	600,000	700,000	100,000	Favourable
Less costs:				
Direct materials	250,000	280,000	30,000	Adverse
Direct wages	100,000	120,000	20,000	Adverse
Machine running costs	25,000	30,000	5,000	Adverse
Depreciation	20,000	20,000	—	
Staff salaries	25,000	20,000	5,000	Favourable
Rent and rates	30,000	30,000	—	
General administration	20,000	15,000	5,000	Favourable
Advertising	5,000	7,000	2,000	Adverse
Others	10,000	13,000	3,000	Adverse
	485,000	535,000	50,000	Adverse
Operating profit	115,000	165,000	50,000	Favourable

As you can probably see from the figures above, a **favourable variance** indicates that:

■ actual sales are greater than budgeted sales; or
■ actual costs are less than budgeted costs.

An **adverse variance** indicates that:

■ actual sales are less than budgeted sales; or
■ actual costs are greater than budgeted costs.

In the example budgetary control report Sales – Costs = Operating profit.

You read just now that managers responsible for different budgets would periodically receive a budgetary control report, and would then be expected to account for variances. Usually senior management would be concerned with adverse variances but favourable variances may also need investigation in case short cuts have been taken to arrive at the apparent advantageous situation, or to learn from it for the future.

Activity 24

Refer back to the budgetary control report for the manufacturing company, shown above.

Below is a list of the managers who receive a copy. Against each job title state the variance which you think each of them would have to account for.

Purchasing manager (reports to factory manager)

_____

Factory manager

_____

Marketing manager

_____

You should have identified that the managers would have to account for the adverse variances as follows.

■ Purchasing manager: direct materials.
■ Factory manager: direct materials, direct wages, machine running costs.
■ Marketing manager: advertising.

You may have felt that the variance of £3000 under 'Others' would have to be investigated, too. As we saw in the budget preparation statement, problems are likely to be inter-related, so that what happens in one area may be the result of a decision made in another area.

It is worth also investigating the sales variance as something might be gained for other aspects of the business from the successes being achieved here. The same can also be said in the areas of staff salaries and general administration where the favourable variances are significant.

Managers may not always be able to take action about variances, whether favourable or adverse. This is because:

■ some costs will be non-controllable;
■ some costs may arise in the budget centre but the responsibility may lie elsewhere. For example, idle time in one department may be caused by the failure of another department to supply information or materials.

Activity 25

15
mins

This Activity may provide the basis of appropriate evidence for your S/NVQ portfolio. If you are intending to take this course of action, it might be better to write your answers on separate sheets of paper.

Think about your own organization.

a To whom do you report variances from budgets and how quickly do you need to report?

_____

_____

_____

b Who, if anyone, reports variances to you?

_____

_____

_____

c Why is it important for variances to be reported as required by your organization? How well are reports of variances followed up; are the causes always sought?

_____

_____

_____

_____

Your response will be related to your own job.

You are likely to report variances to your immediate line manager within a period depending on the significance of the variance. A major problem will require immediate reporting. In the same way, others may report to you.

The speed and extent of reporting depends on organizational policy and the trust you and your colleagues have in each other to deal with problems. You will presumably be able to take action on variances and take control of appropriate resources under your control, or make recommendations to your manager.

2.1 Non-controllable costs

Let's look a little more closely at what we mean by non-controllable costs. These are costs that are charged to a **budget centre**, the name given to a section of business on which a budget is built such as sales or production, but which cannot be influenced by the actions of the people responsible for that budget centre.

Activity 26

Identify **one** example of what you think is a non-controllable cost that might be charged to the budget of your work area.

Here are some examples which came readily to my mind. I hope you can see that they are outside a manager's control.

■ A portion of the rates charged to a departmental budget for the premises it occupies.
■ Diesel fuel costs charged against the transport manager's budget where oil shortages cause prices to soar.
■ Heating costs in a work area where the heating system is controlled centrally.

Since these are outside the control of the manager or supervisor concerned, it's important to identify them separately. Let's look at why this is important.

Activity 27

■ Margaret Shaw is the supervisor of a school canteen with a monthly wages budget of £2000. She receives a budget control report which tells her that the expenditure in her canteen for January, February and March has been £2250 for each month.

Here are the reasons for overspending.

■ January: extra staff employed to cover sickness.
■ February: staff overtime to meet rearranged schedules during school examinations.
■ March: implementation of a nationally agreed bonus scheme, which was not built into the budget.

We usually regard wages as a controllable cost. But is that entirely true in this case?

Decide whether the adverse variance in each month has been caused by controllable or non-controllable wages costs, and note briefly the reason for your decision.

	Controllable	Non-controllable	Reason
January	☐	☐	_____ _____
February	☐	☐	_____ _____
March	☐	☐	_____ _____

> Burton plc examined its costs and changed fixed costs to variable costs by dismissing many of its full-time shop workers and re-employing them as part timers.

Compare your answers with mine.

- January's variance is **non-controllable**. A reasonable allowance for sickness should be built into the budget. Extra cost caused by excessive sickness could hardly be controlled by the supervisor.
- February's cost, however, is **controllable**. The supervisor should have anticipated this problem. Overtime costs for predictable events would certainly be regarded as being within the supervisor's control.
- March's extra costs are clearly **non-controllable**. National agreements lie outside the supervisor's control, and the budget will need to be adjusted to incorporate the extra payment.

We've said that it's important to discover who and what is responsible for any budget variance. This isn't a question of looking for someone to blame. The real issue is finding out why the variance has happened so that corrective action can be taken if necessary.

At the beginning of this session we looked for reasons why there might be a variance on sales and decided that the two likely causes are:

- the quantity sold is different from the quantity budgeted;
- the selling price is different from the price budgeted.

So we can say that sales variances may be caused by:

- volume
- price.

In order to plan what to do next, you need to know the precise cause of the variance. The following situation will show you what I mean.

41

Activity 28

3 mins

■ Unique Double Glazing plans to sell 1000 window units at £200 each. Actual sales are 1100 units, but the price has to be reduced to £175 each.

Calculate the sales variance.

I've already entered some of the information you need to get you started.

Budgeted sales revenue = 1000 × £200 = _____

Actual sales revenue = _____ = £175 = _____

Sales variance = _____ (A/F)

Your calculations should show an adverse sales variance of £7500. Here is how I arrived at that figure.

Budgeted sales revenue = 1000 × £200 = £200,000.
Actual sales revenue = 1100 × £175 = £192,500.
Sales variance = £7500 (A).

In itself, that sales variance doesn't give us the whole picture although you can see from the facts so far that not only has Unique Double Glazing sold another 100 units, it has been unwise enough to drop the price so much as to lose income from the extra sales.

Looking at this in terms of variances. we know that there is:

■ a volume variance – 100 units more than planned were sold;
■ a price/variance – units were sold at £25 less than the budgeted price.

So the variance is actually made up like this:

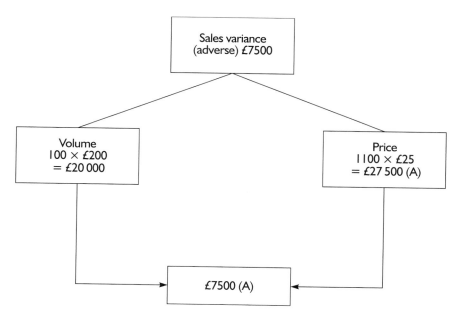

Having broken down the causes of the sales variance, the company would then need to discover the underlying reasons.

Perhaps, in this case, the unit price was reduced because of competition from another supplier, or because extra discount was offered to special customers. There could be all sorts of reasons.

We've seen that it's important to analyse sales variances by:

- volume
- price.

We can analyse any variance on costs in a similar way.

Activity 29

Suppose Unique Double Glazing have an adverse variance on the cost of glass. Jot down the **two** headings under which you think those cost variances could be analysed.

_____

_____

You may not have used the same words as I have but anything on similar lines is acceptable.

- Volume

  Did the business need more glass than budgeted to produce the window units?

- Expenditure

  Did it have to pay more for the glass than budgeted?

All types of costs can be analysed in this way but we're just going to concentrate on two:

- labour
- materials.

Activity 30

8 mins

A job is budgeted to take 50 hours and the rate per hour is £3·00. The actual hours taken are 55 and the hourly rate paid is £3·10.

Calculate the labour cost variance and suggest **two** reasons which you think might have caused the variances in time and the rate.

Budgeted cost = _____ × _____ = _____

Actual cost = _____ × _____ = _____

Variance = _____ (A/F)

Here are my calculations to compare with yours.

Budgeted cost = 50 × £3·00 = £150.
Actual cost = 55 × £3·10 = £170·50.
Variance = £20·50 (A).

We can break that down like this.

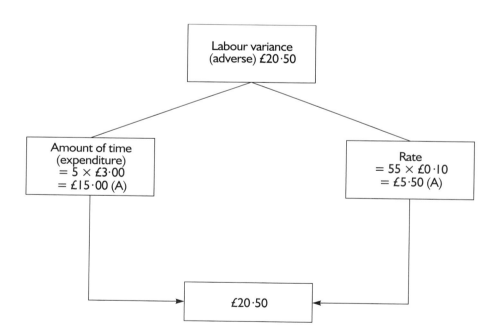

You may have suggested some of the following for the causes of the variances.

Hours (expenditure) variance might be caused by:

- slack work practices resulting from poor supervision;
- machine breakdowns;
- technical problems;
- bottle-necks, leading to material shortages.

Rate variance might be caused by:

- overtime or bonus payments;
- unbudgeted pay award.

Now let's look at a materials variance.

Activity 31

5 mins

■ A job is budgeted to use 1000 kilos of material at £3·00 per kilo.

The actual usage is 1200 kilos, but the price is £2·50 per kilo.

Calculate the material cost variance, and analyse that into the price and expenditure variances. Write your answers on this diagram.

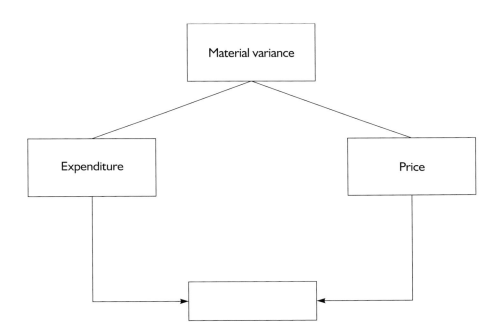

The answer to this Activity can be found on page 74.

45

3 Flexible budgets and budgetary control

In what we have said about budgetary control so far, we have assumed that we were using fixed budgets.

This means that, before the beginning of the period to which the budget relates, costs are budgeted for, and the budgeted costs remain the standard against which actual costs are compared, regardless of what happens during the budget period.

By using a **flexible budget**, on the other hand, we can make adjustments to costs if production and sales vary from the original budget.

A flexible budget is defined by the Chartered Institute of Management Accountants as:

'a budget which is designed to change in accordance with the level of activity attained'.

A flexible budget in fact consists of a series of budgets. Each one is based on a different level of sales or output. As an example, a company might budget for three possible levels of output; costs are then calculated for each level.

Despite the extra effort required in preparing these, flexible budgets can be very useful. Modern computer technology certainly enables flexible budgets to be prepared far more easily and cheaply than drawing them up by hand.

The first thing we have to do is to analyse costs into:

- **fixed costs**, which do not vary with production and sales;
- **variable costs**, which do vary with production and sales.

Let's look at the difference this makes in practice.

Suppose we first assume that all costs are variable; that is, that they will vary in line with sales and production. If we predict that production and sales will fall within the range of 2000–3000 units, we can work out the costs for both these figures. Suppose each unit costs £5. Then the total costs for 2000 units will be £10,000 and the total costs for 3000 units will be £15,000.

The flexible budget would then look like this:

	Budget 1	Budget 2
Production/sales	2000 units	3000 units
Costs	£10,000	£15,000

In this case, the 2000 units in Budget 1 is the lowest expected production/sales figure; the 3000 units in Budget 2 is the highest expected figure. The actual figures are expected to fall somewhere in between these two.

46

In the budgetary control report, assuming sales turn out to be within the expected range, the budget figure written in for sales will be the same as the actual figure. The actual cost can then be compared with the expected costs for that figure. In the case above, the budgetary control report might appear as:

	Budget	Actual	Variance
Production/sales	2500 units	2500 units	
Costs	£12,500	£12,000	£500 (F)

Here the actual sales turned out to be 2500 units (which is within the budgeted range), so the expected costs are 2500 × £5 = £12,500. The actual costs were £500 less than this, so the variance is favourable.

Of course, not all costs are in practice variable; there are always some fixed costs.

Activity 32

6 mins

Let's assume that we regard 50 per cent of our costs as fixed and 50 per cent as variable. The fixed costs are £5000.

Complete the flexible budget and the budgetary control report in this instance.

Flexible budget

	Budget 1	Budget 2
Production/sales	2000 units	3000 units
Costs	£10,000	

Budgetary control report

	Budget	Actual	Variance
Production/sales	2700 units	2700 units	
Costs		£13,000	

As half the costs, i.e. £5000, were fixed, they remain the same, whatever the level of sales. The variable costs for 2000 units, given in Budget 1, must therefore also be £5000 (£10,000 – £5000). This means that variable costs must be £2·50 per unit (£5000 ÷ 2000 units).

The variable costs for Budget 2 are then:

£2·50 × 3000 units = £7500

So the total costs for Budget 2 are:

£5000 fixed costs + £7500 variable costs = £12,500

The completed table is therefore as follows:

Flexible budget

	Budget 1	Budget 2
Production/sales	2000 units	3000 units
Costs	£10,000	£12,500

Turning to the control report, the actual sales are 2700 units. We work out the costs as:

£5000 fixed + (£2·50 × 2700) = £11,750.

This gives a favourable variance of £1250 (£13,000 – £11,750). So the completed table should look like this:

Budgetary control report

	Budget	Actual	Variance
Production/sales	2700 units	2700 units	
Costs	£13,000	£11,750	£1250 (F)

Flexible budgeting is helpful to management in a wide variety of organizations where it is important to be able to take account of changes in circumstances.

Flexible budgets are particularly useful at:

- the planning stage;
- the end of the budget period to revise figures to match reality and to plan for the future.

Using flexible budgets at the planning stage lets you consider the consequences of output being greater or less than expected, within a certain range.

So, if your planned output and sales are 10,000 units, flexible budgeting will allow you to consider in advance what will be the implications of achieving only 8000, or what will be the opportunities of achieving 12,000 units.

Activity 33

5 mins

The outpatient department of a busy district hospital plans for 25,000 outpatient visits a year. Resources — doctors, nurses, secretarial back-up, waiting rooms, etc. — are geared to cope with 25,000 visits. Management use flexible budgeting to consider in advance the problems associated with there being 20,000 or 30,000 visits.

Identify **three** problems which might be anticipated if there are as many as 30,000 visits.

_____

_____

_____

The problems may appear endless. Among these are:

- failure to meet agreed service standards;
- over-tired doctors and other staff;
- overcrowding;
- increased litigation.

A flexible budget will show what the cost implications are across the board resulting from a change so that managers can:

- think ahead
- anticipate problems
- arrive at possible solutions.

4 Other uses of budgeting

Now let's look at how budgeting can be used in the profit planning process.

A simple technique called **break-even analysis** is widely used by all kinds of organizations.

This determines the level of production and sales a business needs to break even – that is, to make no profit but no loss.

Every unit produced and sold above break-even results in profit.	Every unit below break-even results in a loss.

To use break-even analysis to plan profits, we have to break costs down, as we have already done, into **fixed costs** and **variable costs**.

Let's see how it would work.

- Unique Double Glazing budget to sell 1000 window units at £200 each.

  Budgeted fixed cost (rates, management salaries, machine maintenance etc.) are £50,000. Variable costs (materials, direct wages etc.) per window are £100 per unit.

We can forecast the following.

- Each window unit sold adds £200 to income but £100 to costs (the £50,000 fixed costs will exist no matter what the level of sales). The £100 surplus on each window unit sold is called **contribution**.

- When the surplus from each window unit sold matches the fixed cost, break-even point has been reached.

In our example, we have the following:

fixed costs = £50,000

surplus (contribution) per unit = £100

$$\text{break even point} = \frac{£50,000}{£100} = 500 \text{ units}$$

If the company sells 500 units, which is 50 per cent of its target, it will have broken even. If it sells more, it will make a profit: if it sells fewer, it will make a loss.

Remember, the company budgets to sell 1000 units, and profit is sales minus fixed and variable costs.

Activity 34

Calculate the business target profit for Unique Double Glazing if budgeted sales are achieved.

_____

_____

_____

_____

_____

_____

_____

I hope your calculations worked out something like this.

Sales		1000 × £200		£200,000
Less:	Variable costs	1000 × £100	£100,000	
	Fixed costs		£50,000	£150,000
Profit				£50,000

We can also express this as:

500 units above break-even × £100 (surplus) = £50,000.

Activity 35

6 mins

What will be the profit if Unique Double Glazing sells:

a 600 units?

_____

_____

_____

b 400 units?

_____

_____

_____

a If the business sells 600 units, that is 100 units more than the break-even point. The profit will then be 100 × £100 = £10,000 profit.

b If sales only reach 400 units, that is 100 units below break-even, the business will make a loss of 100 × £100 = £10,000 loss.

This technique is useful in helping to make:

- comparisons of production methods;
- deciding what price to charge to easily meet the break-even point and make a profit;
- deciding whether to make something yourself or to buy it in;
- close-down decisions (whether to stop producing goods, provide services and so on, which do not break-even).

Let's look at the first of these points in more detail.

4.1 Comparison of production methods

Let's assume a company sells a product for £40·00 and expects to sell 15,000 units.

There are two ways of making the product.

- Method A is labour intensive (i.e. more staff, fewer machines) with:

  - variable costs = £28 per unit
  - fixed costs = £100,000.

- Method B is labour saving (fewer staff, more machines) with:

  - variable costs = £16 per unit,
  - fixed costs = £250,000.

We want to determine which method:

- is more profitable;
- breaks even at the lower level of sales.

	Labour intensive	Labour saving
Profitability		
Sales 15,000 × £40·00	600,000	600,000
Less variable costs	420,000 (15,000 × £28·00)	240,000 (15,000 × £16·00)
Surplus (contribution)	180,000	360,000
Less fixed costs	100,000	250,000
Profit	80,000	110,000
Break-even		
Selling price	40·00	40·00
Variable costs	28·00	16·00
Surplus (contribution) per unit sold	12·00	24·00
Fixed costs	£100,000	£250,000

Break-even

$$\frac{£100,000}{12·00} = 8333 \text{ units}$$

$$\frac{£250,000}{24·00} = 10,417 \text{ units}$$

Activity 36

If the company is not confident that it can sell 15,000 units, would you recommend Method A or Method B? Give a brief reason for your choice.

_____

_____

_____

If the company is uncertain that it can reach target sales, it would be better off using the labour intensive Method A, which breaks even at a lower figure than Method B.

If, on the other hand, the company had been confident about reaching the target sales, it could well have gone for Method B which offers a bigger profit.

This technique lets management make an **informed** decision about the best production method.

Activity 37

■ The County Council Schools Meals Service has informed all school meals supervisors that their individual meals service must break even or be closed down and replaced by private contractors.

Isabel Smith, a school meal supervisor, can produce and sell a maximum of 1000 meals per week.

She is told her weekly fixed overheads are £1000. County policy is to charge £0·75 per meal and Isabel cannot alter this.

She calculates that the variable costs per meal, mainly raw materials, are £0·25.

Work out the break-even for Isabel's canteen.

$$\frac{\text{Fixed overheads}}{\text{Contribution}} = \underline{\hspace{2cm}} = \underline{\hspace{1.5cm}} \text{ meals}$$

We can see that Isabel's position is fairly desperate! Here are her break-even calculations.

$$\frac{£1000}{£0.50} = 2000 \text{ meals.}$$

She cannot produce 2000 meals because her limit is 1000. Unless she is allowed drastically to increase prices, close-down seems inevitable.

If she could raise her prices to £1·25, her surplus would be £1·00 per meal and if she could sell her maximum number of meals (1000), she would just break even.

Portfolio
of evidence
B1.1, B1.2

Activity 38

This Activity may provide the basis of appropriate evidence for your S/NVQ portfolio. If you are intending to take this course of action, it might be better to write your answers on separate sheets of paper.

Have you been faced with such a problem as described above requiring you to control your resources or make recommendations for the use of your resources so that costs can be cut?

Write down the tasks you had to complete and the reasons you were given for the changes needed.

_____

_____

_____

_____

_____

Your response will be related to your own job.

Perhaps you had to contribute to a decision whether a member of your workteam should be made redundant or to think about whether a new piece of equipment would prove cheaper than one or two new people in the long term.

4.2 Non-financial budgets

Let's look briefly at non-financial budgets. All the budgets we've looked at so far have been concerned with money, but we can use the same techniques to help us plan for other key factors.

Here, for example, is how they can be used to provide information for management decisions on the allocation of resources in a hospital.

Medical specialism	Beds available	Occupancy (%)
Surgery	80	75
Medical	105	80
Geriatric	110	94
Maternity	38	89
Gynaecology	20	80

Now this may not appear like a budget, but the hospital managers are:

- planning for bed usage;
- recording their resources (beds);
- recording the actual outcome (percentage occupancy);
- presumably using the information for future plans.

Activity 39

2 mins

Take a look at the above table.

- Which service is most efficiently managed?

- Which service may be worth reducing?

Geriatric beds are occupied 94 per cent of the time and are used very efficiently. Compared with this, surgery beds are only 75 per cent occupied and this may indicate that the service could be reduced.

Of course, the 'beds available figure' is just the tip of the planning iceberg. Allocating new beds implies that more nursing staff, medical staff and back-up resources will need to be allocated to the specialist areas. Percentage occupancy figures do not indicate costs.

So, you can see the budget process can help manage in a wide range of areas; it need not be restricted to financial statements.

5 Standard costing and budgetary control

Standard costing is really a continuation of budgetary control. Let's see what it is and how it relates to budgetary control.

Here is how the Chartered Institute of Management Accountants defines standard cost:

Standard cost is a predetermined calculation of how much costs should be under specified working conditions and standard costing is therefore a system which uses standards for costs (and revenue) to allow detailed control by the use of variances.

Using standard costs enables us to work out what performance **should** be under certain conditions, so that we can identify variances and so control actual performance.

Perhaps this sounds rather similar to what we have already said about budgeting, particularly using fixed budgets.

Both standard costing and budgeting are:

■ concerned with setting performance standards for the future;
■ aids to control.

They are not, however, the same thing.

The important difference is that:

■ budgets are concerned with totals – such as the costs of an entire department;
■ standard costs are concerned with individual units; each item of production, for instance, will have a standard cost.

Activity 40

If standard costing is concerned with individual units, do you think that this involves more or fewer people in budgetary control than in budgeting? Give reasons for your answer.

_____

_____

Standard costing takes budgetary control 'further down the line', and involves more people in having responsibility for meeting standards in their particular area of work. The advantages of having people involved are:

- if unit costs are applied widely and lots of people are monitoring them, it is possible to identify variances on a much wider range of items, so improving control;
- the setting of standards gives everybody a target to aim for and is likely to make more people cost conscious.

Standard costing, largely controlled by people, means that a lot of information about performance comes in.

This in turn leads to two other advantages of standard costing.

- It's possible to achieve real economies through thinking in advance about the best materials to use, the best methods and so on.
- Attention can be concentrated on the variances which **exceed** predetermined limits, rather than looking at all variances, some of which may be quite minor.

Perhaps we can sum all that up by saying that you don't **have to** use standard costing to achieve budgetary control, but budgetary control is generally more effective if you do.

Self-assessment 3

1 List **five** basic steps of budgetary control systems.

_____

_____

_____

_____

_____

2 State what is indicated by favourable and adverse variances.

_____

_____

_____

_____

3 Identify whether the following are controllable or non-controllable costs.

	Controllable	Non-controllable
a The produce purchased and sold by a greengrocer.	☐	☐
b The rent of a chair in a hairdressing salon.	☐	☐

4 Prizewinning Blooms expects to sell 100 bunches of red roses at £8·50 per bunch on Valentine's day. Sales are hit by a newspaper promotion of chocolates and the business is only able to sell 90 bunches by reducing them to £7·00 per bunch.

Calculate the sales variance and indicate if it is favourable or adverse.

_____

_____

_____

5 Jack Simmons has received an estimate for painting a room of £112, being 16 hours at £7·00. As the painter was unable to complete the job and a less qualified person completed it, the actual cost was for 21 hours at £5·00 per hour.

Calculate the labour cost variance and indicate if it is favourable or adverse.

_____

_____

_____

6   Briefly explain why flexible budgeting is useful to management.

_____

_____

7   A local theatre group has fixed costs of £200. It sells tickets for £5·00 each of which £3·00 is taken up by variable costs. How many tickets must the group sell to break even?

_____

_____

Answers to these questions can be found on page 73.

6 Summary

- Budgets must be put to use to achieve optimum results in organizations, in order to justify the time and effort involved in preparing them.

- Budgetary control allows for the identification and analysis of variances.

- Managers are held responsible for cost variances if these costs are within their control.

- Budgetary control can be achieved through fixed or flexible budgets but flexible budgets are more useful.

- Break-even analysis is a useful addition to the budgeting process and is particularly valuable in profit planning.

- Non-financial budgets can still provide management with useful information.

- Budgetary control is improved by a system of costing such as standard costing.

Performance checks

Write down your answers in the space below to the following questions on *Working with Budgets*.

Question 1 Describe what is meant by a budget.

_____

_____

Question 2 State **three** things shown by a cash budget.

_____

_____

_____

Question 3 What is likely to be the most common budget in an established organization?

_____

Question 4 A budget is of value because it can be used to control activities. What is compared with planned outcome to achieve this?

_____

Question 5 Who would have the responsibility, in a large organization, for the costs of keeping, taking on or shedding staff?

_____

Question 6 An organization plans to sell 6000 units in the next year and to decrease its stock levels by 300 units. What is the required production for the year?

_____

Question 7 Name an organization that uses bed occupancy as a limiting factor.

_____

Question 8 Give another name for a budgeted profit and loss account and budgeted balance sheet.

_____

61

Question 9   What is meant by a variance?

_____

_____

Question 10   Briefly explain what is meant by non-controllable costs.

_____

_____

_____

Question 11   Sales of 200 units at £150 a week are expected. In the first week, a strong demand meant that 250 units were actually sold at £160. Calculate the sales variance and indicate if it is favourable or adverse.

_____

_____

_____

Question 12   Briefly explain the difference between fixed and variable costs.

_____

_____

Question 13   State the formula used to calculate the break-even point.

_____

_____

Question 14   State the difference between budgets and standard costs.

_____

_____

Question 15   Why is standard costing likely to make more people cost conscious?

_____

_____

_____

Answers to these questions can be found on page 75.

2 Workbook assessment

Read the following case incident and then deal with the questions that follow, writing your answers on a separate sheet of paper.

- Dickens Ltd manufactures a single product. Here is the company's budgeted performance for the month of March.

Production budget:

Sales	20,000 units at £10·00

Direct materials	£60,000
Direct labour	£40,000
Maintenance	£10,000
Supervisory wages	£25,000
Rent and rates	£25,000
Other costs	£36,000

Production actual:

Sales	37,500 units at £8·00

Direct materials	£85,000
Direct labour	£45,000
Maintenance	£14,000
Supervisory wages	£27,000
Rent and rates	£26,000
Other costs	£50,000

1 Produce a budgetary control report comparing:

a budgeted to actual sales;
b budgeted to actual costs;
c budgeted to actual profit.

Remember that every variance should be followed by (F) Favourable or (A) Adverse.

2 Show how the sales revenue variance can be broken down into:

a sales price
b sales volume.

3 Suppose in the above budgeted information the following cost information was available:

a direct materials, direct labour and maintenance costs are regarded as variable;

b rent and rates and supervisory wages are regarded as fixed;

c other costs consist of fixed costs (£16,000) and variable costs (£1·00 per unit produced and sold).

Produce a budgetary control report which takes into account this information about fixed and variable costs.

4 Briefly say what you think the advantages of a flexible budget system would be in this case.

3 Work-based assignment

The time guide for this assignment gives you an approximate idea of how long it is likely to take you to write up your findings. You will need to spend some additional time gathering information perhaps talking to colleagues and thinking about the assignment. The result of your efforts should be presented on separate sheets of paper.

Your written response to this Assignment may provide the basis of appropriate evidence for your S/NVQ portfolio.

There may be some form of budgetary control in your workplace.

Describe the system used for budgets, and any standard costing used in your workplace. Identify any shortcomings in the present system and think of ways these might be improved without damaging the successful aspects of the system.

Explain to your immediate manager and your workteam that you are researching budgetary control in your workplace, discuss your ideas with them and make a note of their suggestions and objections to change.

Draw up a report covering the following questions.

1 Who has direct responsibility for the budget in your work area and to whom is that person directly responsible?

2 Which budget or budgets are you or your manager responsible for producing?

3 Describe how information about actual performance (e.g. actual costs) is fed back to you and your workteam.

4   Do you think the feedback of information to you could be improved so that you could be more involved in budgetary control? If so, briefly suggest how this could be done.

5   Describe what happens if actual performance does not correspond to budget. Are you or your workteam held to be responsible in any way?

6   How do you feel resources can be better managed?

7   How can changes to the budgetary control system be introduced with the minimum of objections?

If there doesn't appear to be a clear budgetary control system in your workplace, and you would find it difficult to answer the questions above, describe how you think a budgetary control system could be set up in your workplace.

Write up your findings and draw up an action plan for you and your workteam. Discuss this with your manager.

Reflect and review

1 Reflect and review

Now that you have completed your work on *Working with Budgets*, let us review our workbook objectives.

The first objective is:

■ that you should be better able to describe what a budget is.

We've seen that a budget is a financial plan prepared in advance of a certain period. Every department in a business organization is involved in forecasting its budget depending on the level of business activity planned. This can involve a lot of work, but can be a worthwhile investment if the budget is regarded, not as a financial straight-jacket, but as a valuable management tool for planning and controlling.

■ As a first line manager, can you think of improvements in planning and control in your work area that you could suggest to your manager? Make notes of any matters which come to mind below.

_____

_____

_____

_____

_____

■ What are the advantages of budgeting to you and your workteam? Make a note of these if you feel you need to emphasize these.

_____

_____

_____

The second workbook objective was:

■ that you should be better able to provide the information required to prepare budgets.

We've discovered that the preparation of the budget, the planning stage, is every bit as important as operating within the budget once it is set. At this stage, management are very dependent on the quality and accuracy of the

67

information you give them. I hope you'll find that a better understanding of how costs are broken down, and of how budgets actually operate will help you to provide and understand the budget information you are asked for.

- Do you feel that you prepare information in the most effective way? And is the information the most useful to those who use it? If you can think of changes which would improve the quality of information you supply, write your thoughts below so you can refer to them for later discussions at work.

_____

_____

_____

_____

_____

- Is there other information available in your work area that you do not presently supply for budgeting purposes which should be available? Note down your thoughts for future reference.

_____

_____

_____

The third workbook objective was:

- that you should be better able to understand how budgets are used.

A budget is an expensive exercise unless it is constantly used during the period it relates to. We've seen that it can be used to compare actual performance with planned performance, flexed to take into account changes in circumstances or to forecast what will happen in certain circumstances and to make plans accordingly. It also helps management to determine the point at which they will begin to make a profit, by the use of break-even analysis, and thus to set targets which ensure the profitability of the organization.

- Can you think of ways to improve the way budgets are used in your workplace? Make a note of any suggestions you have for change.

_____

_____

_____

- Are any budgets you use at work flexed to an appropriate extent? Write down your thoughts for future discussions with your manager.

_____

_____

_____

The final workbook objective was:

■ that you should be able to use some budgetary control techniques.

Using fairly simple examples, we've used some budgetary control techniques which would be used in your workplace. These include break-even analysis, flexible budgeting and standard costing which we have only mentioned in this workbook. If you are involved in setting the budget in your work area or are on a budget committee, the work you have done in this workbook should have increased the confidence with which you handle the techniques.

■ Make a note of techniques you could use in assisting your planning and control.

---

2 Action plan

Use this plan to further develop for yourself a course of action you want to take. Make a note in the left-hand column of the issues or problems you want to tackle, and then decide what you intend to do, and make a note in Column 2.

The resources you need might include time, materials, information or money. You may need to negotiate for some of them, but they could be something easily acquired, like half an hour of somebody's time, or a chapter of a book. Put whatever you need in Column 3. No plan means anything without a timescale, so put a realistic target completion date in Column 4.

Finally, describe the outcome you want to achieve as a result of this plan, whether it is for your own benefit or advancement, or a more efficient way of doing things.

69

Desired outcomes

1 Issues

2 Action

3 Resources

4 Target completion

Actual outcomes

3 Extensions

Extension 1

Book   *The Business Plan Workbook*
Authors   Colin Barrow, Paul Barrow and Robert Brown
Edition   Second edition, revised 1995
Publisher   Kogan Page

Extension 2

Book   *Accounting for Non-accountants*
Author   Graham Mott
Edition   Fourth edition 1993
Publisher   Kogan Page

Extension 3

Book   *Budgeting for Business*
Author   Leon Hopkins
Edition   First edition 1994
Publisher   Kogan Page

Extension 4

Book   *Successful Budgeting in a Week*
Author   Malcolm Secrett
Edition   First edition 1993
Publisher   Hodder & Stoughton

These Extensions can be taken up via your NEBS Management Centre. They will arrange for you to have access to them. However, it may be more convenient to check out the materials with your personnel or training people at work – they could well give you access. There are good reasons for approaching your own people as, by doing so, they will become aware of your continuing interest in the subject and you will be able to involve them in your development.

4 Answers to self-assessment questions

Self-assessment 1 on page 11

1 The four features of a budget are that it:
- is quantitative;
- is prepared in advance;
- relates to a particular period;
- is a plan of action;

2 Budgets are essential for deciding at the outset whether an objective can be achieved and what this requires. They also give managers their targets and cost limits for the next period.

71

3 a Budgets are largely a waste of time unless they are actively USED in order to see whether the organization is MEETING its targets and keeping within its limits.

This helps to ensure that expenditure takes place according to plan.

b We use the term BUDGETARY CONTROL to cover the use of budgets to help an organization control its progress towards what it has set out to achieve.

Setting targets and encouraging people to adhere to them assists the organization through a disciplined approach.

c A budget will not be useful to an organization if it is managed so RIGIDLY that it does not permit some degree of flexibility.

Unless allowances are made for changes in circumstances, organizations can incur expenses and losses in trying to achieve the impossible.

Self-assessment 2 on page 32

1 a The KEY or LIMITING factor is the factor on which all other budgets depend.

This can be sales or production levels, cash or other aspects which mean that an organization cannot trade at a higher level without attention to the key factor itself.

b A budget committee is usually made up of people who represent major areas of RESPONSIBILITY over expenditure.

Responsibility for expenditure promotes proper use of budgets.

2 The planned production level is calculated as follows.

Sales 12,000 + 10% (1200) = 13,200 units

13,200 units less planned decrease in stock levels of 680 (2000 − 1320) = 12,520 units

3 a Details of birth rates and local housing starts and (c) National pay awards are EXTERNAL sources of information, (b) Advice from teachers about the need for new books and equipment is INTERNAL.

4 Poor supervision of labour leads to poor timekeeping; of machine use leads to breakdowns; and of materials usage can lead to pilferage.

5 Organizations maintain departmental budgets to define costs and responsibilities to specific cost centres.

Self-assessment 3 on page 58

1   The five basic steps of budgetary control systems are to :

- establish agreed budgets;
- report actual results to departmental managers;
- identify where actual performance differs from planned performance using variances;
- agree which department or who is responsible for variances;
- analyse why variances have happened.

2   A favourable variance indicates that actual sales are greater than budgeted sales, or actual costs are less than budgeted costs. An adverse variance indicates that actual sales are less than budgeted sales, or actual costs are greater than budgeted costs.

3   a   The produce purchased and sold by a greengrocer are controllable costs.

   b   The rent of a chair in a hairdressing salon is non-controllable.

4   The sales variance is calculated as:

Budgeted sales revenue 100 × £8·50 = £850
Actual sales revenue 90 × £7·00   = £630

Sales variance   £220 adverse

5   The labour cost variance is:

Budgeted cost 16 × £7·00 = £112
Actual cost 21 × £5·00   = £105

Variance   £7 favourable

6   Flexible budgeting provides the opportunity to be able to take account of changes in circumstances and more closely monitor the position than is possible using fixed budgets.

7   The break-even point is $\dfrac{£200}{£5 - £3}$ = 100 tickets.

5 Answers to activities

Activity 16 on page 23

You may not have used exactly the same budget titles as me, but the sequence of budget preparation should be similar to the following

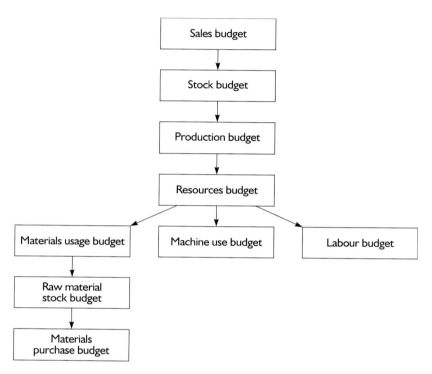

Activity 31 on page 45

Budgeted material cost = 1000 kilos × £3·00 = £3000.
Actual material cost = 1200 kilos × £2·50 = £3000.
Variance = nil

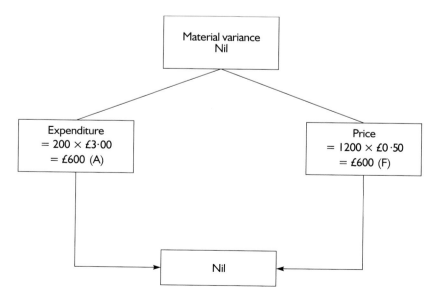

In this case, the lower price exactly counters the extra cost from using 200 kilos more than were budgeted for.

74

5 Answers to the quick quiz

Answer 1　A budget is a quantitative plan of action prepared in advance of a defined period of time.

Answer 2　A cash budget shows:

- the cash received and paid out during the budget period;
- the timing of receipts and payments;
- the bank balance or overdraft for each month.

Answer 3　The sales budget.

Answer 4　Actual outcome.

Answer 5　The human resources/personnel manager.

Answer 6　5700 units.

Answer 7　An hotel or hospital.

Answer 8　Master budget.

Answer 9　The difference between actual and planned performance.

Answer 10　Cost charged to a budget centre, but which cannot be influenced by the activities of people responsible for that budget centre.

Answer 11　Budgeted sales revenue 200 × £150　= £30,000
Actual sales revenue 250 × £160　　= £40,000

Sales variance　　　　　　　　　　　£10,000 favourable

Answer 12　Fixed costs do not vary with sales and production. Variable costs do vary.

Answer 13　Break-even point $= \dfrac{\text{Fixed costs}}{\text{Contribution}}$

Answer 14　Budgets are concerned with totals whereas standard costs are concerned with individual units.

Answer 15　The setting of standards gives everybody a target to aim for.

6 Certificate

Completion of this certificate by an authorized person shows that you have worked through all the parts of this workbook and satisfactorily completed the assessments. The certificate provides a record of what you have done that may be used for exemptions or as evidence of prior learning against other nationally certificated qualifications.

Pergamon Open Learning and NEBS Management are always keen to refine and improve their products. One of the key sources of information to help this process are people who have just used the product. If you have any information or views, good or bad, please pass these on.

NEBS
MANAGEMENT
DEVELOPMENT

SUPER SERIES

THIRD EDITION

Working with Budgets

....

has satisfactorily completed this workbook

Name of signatory ....

Position ....

Signature ....

Date ....

Official stamp

SUPER SERIES

SUPER SERIES 3

0-7506-3362-X   Full Set of Workbooks, User Guide and Support Guide

A. Managing Activities

0-7506-3295-X	1. Planning and Controlling Work
0-7506-3296-8	2. Understanding Quality
0-7506-3297-6	3. Achieving Quality
0-7506-3298-4	4. Caring for the Customer
0-7506-3299-2	5. Marketing and Selling
0-7506-3300-X	6. Managing a Safe Environment
0-7506-3301-8	7. Managing Lawfully - Safety, Health and Environment
0-7506-37064	8. Preventing Accidents
0-7506-3302-6	9. Leading Change

B. Managing Resources

0-7506-3303-4	1. Controlling Physical Resources
0-7506-3304-2	2. Improving Efficiency
0-7506-3305-0	3. Understanding Finance
0-7506-3306-9	4. Working with Budgets
0-7506-3307-7	5. Controlling Costs
0-7506-3308-5	6. Making a Financial Case

C. Managing People

0-7506-3309-3	1. How Organisations Work
0-7506-3310-7	2. Managing with Authority
0-7506-3311-5	3. Leading Your Team
0-7506-3312-3	4. Delegating Effectively
0-7506-3313-1	5. Working in Teams
0-7506-3314-X	6. Motivating People
0-7506-3315-8	7. Securing the Right People
0-7506-3316-6	8. Appraising Performance
0-7506-3317-4	9. Planning Training and Development
0-75063318-2	10. Delivering Training
0-7506-3320-4	11. Managing Lawfully - People and Employment
0-7506-3321-2	12. Commitment to Equality
0-7506-3322-0	13. Becoming More Effective
0-7506-3323-9	14. Managing Tough Times
0-7506-3324-7	15. Managing Time

D. Managing Information

0-7506-3325-5	1. Collecting Information
0-7506-3326-3	2. Storing and Retrieving Information
0-7506-3327-1	3. Information in Management
0-7506-3328-X	4. Communication in Management
0-7506-3329-8	5. Listening and Speaking
0-7506-3330-1	6. Communicating in Groups
0-7506-3331-X	7. Writing Effectively
0-7506-3332-8	8. Project and Report Writing
0-7506-3333-6	9. Making and Taking Decisions
0-7506-3334-4	10. Solving Problems

SUPER SERIES 3 USER GUIDE + SUPPORT GUIDE

0-7506-37056	1. User Guide
0-7506-37048	2. Support Guide

SUPER SERIES 3 CASSETTE TITLES

0-7506-3707-2	1. Complete Cassette Pack
0-7506-3711-0	2. Reaching Decisions
0-7506-3712-9	3. Managing the Bottom Line
0-7506-3710-2	4. Customers Count
0-7506-3709-9	5. Being the Best
0-7506-3708-0	6. Working Together

To Order - phone us direct for prices and availability details
(please quote ISBNs when ordering)
College orders: 01865 314333 • Account holders: 01865 314301
Individual purchases: 01865 314627 (please have credit card details ready)

We Need Your Views

We really need your views in order to make the Super Series 3 (SS3) an even better learning tool for you. Please take time out to complete and return this questionnaire to Tessa Gingell, Pergamon Open Learning, Linacre House, Jordan Hill, Oxford, OX2 8BR.

Name :..

Address :...

....

Company & Position (if applicable) :..

Title of workbook : ....

If applicable, please state which qualification you are studying for. If not, please describe what study you are undertaking, and with which organisation or college:

....

Please grade the following out of 10 (10 being extremely good, 0 being extremely poor):

Content   .... Appropriateness to your position   ....
Readability   .... Qualification coverage   ....

What did you particularly like about this workbook?

Are there any features you disliked about this workbook? Please identify them.

Are there any errors we have missed? If so, please state page number: ....

How are you using the material? For example, as an open learning course, as a reference resource, as a training resource etc.

....

How did you hear about Super Series 3?:

Word of mouth: Through my tutor/trainer: Mailshot:

Other (please give details): ....

Many thanks for your help in returning this form.